Original title:
Life's Secrets: Locked, But Not Forgotten

Copyright © 2025 Creative Arts Management OÜ
All rights reserved.

Author: Jasper Montgomery
ISBN HARDBACK: 978-1-80566-200-6
ISBN PAPERBACK: 978-1-80566-495-6

Enigmatic Echoes

Whispers of socks that roam free,
Chasing each other in wild spree.
Lost keys laugh, bobbing their head,
Hints of mischief, where they tread.

Secrets in drawers, a jumbled fight,
Old candy wrappers taking flight.
Ticklish memories, a giggle or two,
Life's a riddle, but so is my shoe!

The Forgotten Scrolls

Unraveled napkins with doodles galore,
Collecting dust where the pizza once bore.
Ancient takeout menus try to remind,
Of treasures once ordered, now hard to find.

Chapters of awkward, well-penned in sauce,
Each leftover bite, an adventure glossed.
Fridge magnets whisper, 'We had our fun!'
Yet quite like the fridge, we just keep on run.

Beneath the Surface of Time

Under the bed, the monsters conspire,
With crumbs of laughter, they never tire.
Dust bunnies plot a surprise attack,
While old coins complain of a lack.

On the clock's tick-tock, a dance they'll do,
Wobbling tales, mixed up in the woo.
Forgotten socks share deep, dark dreams,
Of socks on a mission, or so it seems.

Chaos of Untold Legends

In the attic reside tales aloof,
Ghostly memories sealed under a roof.
Old toys bicker over who's been played,
While dust settles on the dreams they made.

A tower of books, all mistaken looks,
Fictional brawls in overly crowded nooks.
The cat's the hero, with tales bold and grand,
A fluffy legend, ruler of this land!

The Chamber of Dreams Unrevealed.

In a room where dreams collide,
Laughter echoes side by side.
Whispers tickle, jokes unfold,
Secrets wrapped in threads of gold.

The cat's a spy, or so they say,
With a purr that leads astray.
Pillow forts and giggles soar,
Who knew sleep could offer more?

A sock drawer's a hidden vault,
Where mismatched pairs cause quite a jolt.
Unlock the fun, let the games start,
In this chamber, play the heart.

Remember when we danced with bears?
In pajamas, we faced our fears.
The door may creak, but what's the fuss?
Every laugh's a gift, let's discuss!

Whispers of the Heart

A heart that hums a silly tune,
Whispers love beneath the moon.
In every giggle, a truth appears,
Unlocking joy and drawing cheers.

Kind words float like dandelion seeds,
Planting smiles in friendly deeds.
When in doubt, just share a pun,
And watch the weight of worry run.

Like fortune cookies taking flight,
Their cryptic messages feel just right.
"Your fridge is empty!" seems quite sweet,
When shared with folks who love to eat.

In the hush of laughter's glow,
Secrets spill, their magic flow.
Beneath the laughter, the heart may tease,
As joy unlocks with playful ease.

Hidden Treasures of the Soul

In a treasure chest of giggles bright,
Lies a hoard of pure delight.
Jokes and riddles finely spun,
Hidden gems for everyone.

A cookie jar is the map, you see,
Leading straight to laughter's spree.
Each crumb a clue, each bite a laugh,
Unlocking joy, the better half.

A grumpy cat in a pirate hat,
Claims each laugh has gone splat!
But with a wink, it pounces near,
Proving even grumps hold cheer.

So dive in deep, explore the stash,
Where silliness awaits to clash.
The soul's true treasure isn't gold,
But funny stories yet untold.

The Key Beneath the Surface

Beneath the waves of daily grind,
Lies a key that sparks the mind.
Tickled toes and cosmic chords,
Unlocking laughter, gracious hoards.

Under every serious face,
Lurks a clown, just waits for space.
With silly hats and jumping shoes,
The key is fun, it's what we choose.

A sneeze can set the tension free,
A wink becomes a mystery.
Dial up joy, turn down the stress,
Life's a jest, not a test!

So take a breath, let worries slide,
And let the silly sit inside.
For deep within, we hold the key,
To laughter shared, in harmony.

The Unraveled Mystique

In the attic, dust gathers thick,
Old trunks await with their ancient tricks.
A sock puppet sings a silly song,
While a squeaky frog croaks along.

Nostalgic photos do a dance,
Reminding us of teenage romance.
A secret note in a crumpled page,
Scribbles a plan to act our age.

Whispers of cake from the kitchen rise,
As pies plot mischief with gooey lies.
Laughter ensues, and the cat gives chase,
As secrets escape without a trace.

In each crevice, joy hides with glee,
Clowns in pockets, oh what a spree!
What mysteries lurk in shadows cast,
We find in fun, the future and past.

The Unwhispered Truth

Under the table, a shoe goes missing,
A three-legged cat is slyly kissing.
Pigs in pajamas do jumps and flips,
While unmarked letters take secret trips.

The goldfish mumbles conspiracy plans,
While it dreams of bowling with tiny cans.
A remote control goes on a quest,
To find the snacks, more than a jest.

Upside down socks on the ceiling spin,
As cheerful gnomes play their violin.
Noodles dance with an unkempt do,
Hiding the secrets we never knew.

The clock ticks loudly, the dog does bark,
In the shadows, there's a marvelously spark.
What's true and what is just plain silliness?
In laughter's light, we find our bliss.

Dances in Darkened Corners

Frogs in tuxedos throw a grand ball,
Where dust bunnies waltz and disco ball.
A plant in a pot tries to break free,
Yearning for wild nights under a tree.

An old broom hides tales of the past,
Of every time it was used in a blast.
With fibs tangled in ribbons and lace,
They laugh and spin in a goofy race.

Curiosity tickles a wandering nose,
As crumpled maps lead to hidden prose.
Forgotten toys play peek-a-boo charms,
In nooks and crannies, they wave their arms.

Giggling shadows dance on the wall,
As secrets of joy come to call.
A melodious chime sings of glee,
In darkened corners, we all feel free.

Secrets in the Starlight

Balloons with secrets float in the night,
As cupcakes frolic under the moonlight.
Twinkling stars gossip about the cake,
While clouds drift by with whimsy awake.

Invisible fairies throw a parade,
Twirling on beams where wishes are made.
A tickle fight ensues between friends,
As squishy marshmallows aim for the ends.

Giggles echo through the midnight air,
With each silly whisper, we dance without care.
A treasure map made of candy bars,
Leads us on quests through dreams and stars.

Laughter erupts as the sun starts to gleam,
Remembering secrets and ridiculous schemes.
In starlit moments, the heart stays light,
For silly shenanigans make everything bright.

The Diary of Unanswered Questions

Why did I eat that last piece of cake?
Should I call Bob, or bake a fake?
The sock monster steals without shame,
And why do cats think we're their game?

Journals filled with riddle and rhyme,
Tell me, are they just wasting time?
I search for answers in a happy trance,
But they laugh back at me, a silent dance.

Keys to the Soul's Sanctuary

I've got a key that fits nowhere right,
Found it in my cereal, what a sight!
It jingles in pockets, a comedic sound,
Unlocking nothing but the quirks around.

The doorways of thought, where wishes reside,
Search for the handle, but who's got the guide?
A treasure map drawn on the back of my hand,
Leading me nowhere, yet so very grand.

Mirrors of the Unspoken

In the mirror, my reflections frown,
What do they see? They never come down.
Do they whisper jokes when I am not near?
Or laugh at my socks that don't quite match here?

Unsaid thoughts in a glimmering haze,
Waving back at me in a witty daze.
I nod in reply, play along with the jest,
But only I know who's jesting the best.

Hidden Rooms of Heartfelt Truth

Behind every door lies a mystery bright,
A spoon that's a shovel? Oh, what a delight!
With cupboards that giggle and closets that sigh,
They hide all their treasures—but really, oh why?

Whispers of plush toys carrying tales,
About borrowed socks and mysteriously lost pails.
Exploring these spaces, I chuckle and grin,
For the truth of it all's that we're giggling within.

Forgotten Pages of Yesterday

In a box on the shelf, quite dusty and old,
Stories unfold, yet they've never been told.
A sock that once danced, now just sits and sighs,
While the cat reads a book, with its keen little eyes.

There's a sandwich from lunch, in the depths of a tome,
It whispers of pickles, then vows to go home.
Time travelers laugh at what they find there,
In a world full of wonder, and a few pet cat hairs.

Memories Behind the Glass

Behind the old window, dust bunnies play,
They watch all the people, who hurry away.
A pen from the past dreams of writing a note,
While it stares at the wall like an old-fashioned goat.

The jokes we once laughed at, now seem quite absurd,
Like a bird that forgot how to speak just one word.
Yet the laughter still lingers, like crumbs on the floor,
As we peek behind glass, and remember once more.

Hidden Drops of Time

In the attic we found, a tickle of dust,
A jar full of giggles, the memories rust.
There's a clock that once ticked like a jolly old man,
Now it just snoozes while dreaming of sand.

In this treasure of smiles, with moments that gleam,
A rubber band ball, living out its grand dream.
As whispers of laughter drip out from the seams,
We swim through the past, in a pool of our dreams.

The Safe Within the Heart

A heart-shaped safe hides the giggles of yore,
With candy and secrets and silly folklore.
It holds all the laughter, with a sprinkle of cheer,
And occasionally dines with a forgotten old deer.

When the key gets misplaced, it just chuckles and sighs,
For jokes are the locks in the wink of our eyes.
In this vault of delight, we store all our fun,
As we dance to the beats of the laughter we've spun.

Secrets Beneath the Skin

Oh, my belly's got a riddle,
Wobbling like a worn-out fiddle.
It giggles when I laugh too loud,
A jolly party, far too proud.

In my pocket, change may jingle,
But in my heart, old jokes still dingle.
I swear my shoes have got their quirks,
They dance alone—those sneaky jerks!

My nose knows more than all will say,
It catches scents that drift away.
Crisp cookies caught in a whiff,
That never quite makes it to my lift.

With every wrinkle, a story's spun,
Of midnight snacks and silly fun.
Those secrets scrawled upon my face,
Dance in the light, a goofy grace.

The Archive of Lost Moments

In a drawer, the socks are hiding,
Pairs unmatched, they're all confiding.
Old receipts and ticket stubs,
Of concerts lost in tourist pubs.

Bottled laughter from a rainy day,
Where puddles mirrored skies of gray.
I penned a note, forgot the place,
Now it's just a funny space.

Crayons clutched yet never used,
My art skills, should be amused!
Doodles of a cat in a hat,
Wit's a whisker, imagine that!

Time machines run on iced cream spills,
And working clocks that sing for thrills.
The moments piled, a dizzy heap,
In my heart they forever leap.

Hushed Confessions

Whispers weave through pastel halls,
Crispy chips, oh how it calls!
A secret stash beneath the bed,
Pretending chips are good for spread.

An empty jar, once full of joy,
The prize inside—a sneaky ploy.
Cereal boxes hide the truth,
Their crunch betrays a hidden youth.

Under capes of silence, I chuckle,
My laundry's mute, no hidden buckle.
But oh, the socks that seek escape,
Run wild, they wear a jaunty cape!

Giggling in the soft moonlight,
My fears dissolve, they're out of sight.
The hilarity of a lost shoe,
Adventures told, with shades of blue.

Fragments of Yesterday

A mem'ry box of yesterdays,
Filled with laughter and quirky gaze.
Photos that show a missing tooth,
The ghost of my unfunny youth.

Silly hats and well-worn shoes,
Each a tale of glorious snooze.
Bad hair days that knew no end,
And fruit snacks I'd share with a friend.

I still recall that tropic sun,
Where sunscreen fights an epic run.
My bright pink nose, a beacon bright,
A laugh in every sandy flight.

The pieces puzzle, a joyful mess,
In every glance, a sweet caress.
Each fragment speaks in giggles and cheer,
Echoes of days that stay quite clear.

Threads Woven in Silence

In the attic, dustbunnies play,
Whispering tales of yesterday's clay.
Sock puppets dance, with mismatched glee,
Secrets tucked snug, as snug as can be.

A cat with a hat, looks quite perplexed,
She knows all the dishes, but won't help the texts.
Chasing lost whispers that float in the air,
While moths debate fashion, without a care.

The threadbare rug hums an old tune,
As grandma's yarn spins under the moon.
Knots in the fabric, hidden with cheer,
Woven in laughter, but not very clear.

So raise a toast to the secrets we share,
In pockets and corners, if you dare.
With giggles and grins, life's puzzles we tease,
Unlocked by the laughter, as easy as breeze.

The Secrets We Breathe

In the kitchen, a kettle sings hot,
Its whistle spills secrets, bubbling a lot.
Tomatoes gossip, the peas take a stand,
While onions shed tears, unplanned and unplanned.

A toaster conspires with the jam on the shelf,
Making breakfast dreams, all by itself.
Eggs scramble stories, sunny side up,
While coffee brews fables in a paper cup.

The floorboards creak, as they eavesdrop near,
On tales of socks that have disappeared.
To everywhere they wander, no one will know,
In the world of the lost, where they silently go.

But we breathe those secrets, like fresh baked bread,
Each crumb a reminder of stories well spread.
So sip on the joy, as we feast at this table,
Unraveling secrets, oh, if we are able.

Facets of a Shattered Mirror

A broken mirror shows my worst side,
Reflecting the chaos where secrets reside.
One shard is a smile, the next is a frown,
While the fragments conspire to poke fun all around.

With every glimmer, a riddle unfolds,
In laughter we find what the heart slowly holds.
A tale of a jester dressed in fine thread,
With mismatched intentions, but nothing to dread.

The edges are sharp, but the humor is bright,
In cracks of mischief, we find pure delight.
Each piece tells a story; each facet a dream,
Hidden within, like a whimsical theme.

So gather the fragments, the stories so bold,
Reflecting our laughs, and sometimes our cold.
In this shattered embrace, we find what is true,
The humor in chaos, and laughter anew.

Portals of Past Reflections

Beneath the old porch, the memories stir,
Where fireflies gather, and crickets confer.
Each crack in the wood whispers jokes of yore,
As ghosts in the laughter invite us for more.

With slides of the past playing tag on the wall,
The shadows have stories, all ready to call.
A pair of old glasses, quite dusty and round,
Show visions of mischief that linger around.

The swing creaks softly, like a song on repeat,
With giggles of children, a time bittersweet.
Each push brings the echoes of what used to be,
In the laughter of ages, so wild and so free.

So through these portals, we dance and we glide,
Embracing the moments that won't let us hide.
With humor we savor, these glimpses so bright,
In the tapestry woven, we find pure delight.

Coiled Stories in the Dark

In shadows where giggles hide,
A sock and a shoe, side by side.
Whispers of mischief, oh what a sight,
Tales of the lost, come to light!

Under the bed, dust bunnies play,
With crumbs from last week's buffet array.
A sandwich, long gone, but spirits still roam,
In the dark, they've made it their home!

Old toys with stories, unspoken, unshared,
Wondering and waiting, yet nobody cared.
With each gentle laugh, they'll erode every fear,
In the depth of the night, they still persevere.

So leave the light on, let shadows take flight,
For hidden giggles may spark delight.
These coiled stories, with laughter they bloom,
In the corners of silence, they take up the room.

Masked Promises of Tomorrow

Winks and nods in a hurried disguise,
A promise made under funky pink skies.
With cake on your nose, how can you resist?
Tomorrow's plan shrouded in whipped cream mist!

Sneaky cupcakes, all lined up in rows,
Whispering secrets only dessert knows.
Behind every icing, a cheeky delight,
Masked sweet whispers that tickle the night.

Chasing rainbows in socks, mismatched, it's true,
Each step is a giggle, a bright joyful hue.
Tomorrow's absurdity, all wrapped up tight,
In promises made when the time feels just right.

So let's dance with fate, in our own silly show,
As masked promises swirl, and the cupcakes all glow.
With laughter our armor, we'll grin and we'll sway,
For tomorrow holds wonders, in a whimsical way.

Threads of the Absent

In a cupboard, clothes wait for a spin,
Mismatched socks holding hands in a grin.
A scarf with a tale tangled up tight,
Threads of the absent laugh through the night.

The old chair creaks with memories it boasts,
Of a wayward cat and some ghostly toasts.
Each thread sings of laughter, each fray has a song,
While dust bunnies giggle, 'You don't quite belong!'

With patterns that twist, and colors that clash,
Knitted future dreams in a glorious mash.
The yarn balls conspire, in whispers they scheme,
To spin silly stories, the fabric of dreams.

So gather the threads that have danced through the years,
With laughter and joy, let's dry off our tears.
For even the absent have stories to share,
In whimsical fabric, adorned with a flare!

The Lock that Holds the Past

A tiny vault, with echoes inside,
Each jangle and jolt carries joy, not pride.
The lock is all rusty, but hey, so what?
It guards the giggles, keeps the ruckus in shot!

Keys hang like dreams on a whimsical hook,
One's shaped like a fish, the other a book.
Turning them gently sets chaos afloat,
As past silly antics start to emote.

Mismatched emotions, old photos to tease,
With laughter like breezes that dance through the trees.
Secrets of childhood, in pockets they swell,
In the lock that holds stories, we cherish so well.

So twist every key, feel the rush of the past,
There's fun to be had, if you've got time to last.
For even those memories, once lost, now appear,
In a lock that was rusty, but holds laughter near!

The Lock That Never Was

I bought a lock from a shady shop,
They said it was magic, a real showstop.
But when I tried to use it, oh what a sight,
It turned out to be just a paperweight, right?

I laughed and I chuckled at my foolish buy,
My dreams of treasure had flown up high.
But now it sits pretty on my dusty shelf,
A reminder that treasures can't be bought—only felt.

So next time you find a lock on sale,
Remember my story, don't lose your trail.
For sometimes the key is not made of gold,
It's the laughter we share, the tales we've told.

So here's to the locks that never could hold,
The ones that reveal, rather than control.
Let's jingle the keys, with a grin so wide,
And dance with our secrets, not trying to hide.

Trails of Invisible Ink

With a pen in hand, I wrote a note,
But forgot to refill, no ink would float.
My secrets in shadows, just whispers of fun,
Dancing around, like a shy little nun.

I showed my friend and she giggled with glee,
'Is that a message or just empty spree?'
I winked and I shrugged, 'A masterpiece bright,'
Invisible stories, oh what a delight.

We scribbled more jokes on pages so bare,
Forgotten confessions, floated in the air.
Our minds filled with laughter, as silly thoughts strewn,
Like trails of invisible ink under the moon.

Next time you write, know this one little thing,
Sometimes the blank page can also bring zing.
For laughter and friendship need not be in ink,
They can float on the air, on a wink and a blink.

Fortune Favors the Silent

In a quiet corner, I sat with some stew,
While loud mouths yapped about what they all knew.
But fortune chuckled and winked my way,
While silence served up a buffet—hooray!

I peered at the loud ones, their stories so grand,
But I was the one who got served extra brand.
With a grin on my plate and a wink in my eye,
Silent desires can soar and fly.

We snickered together, my soup and I,
While they clattered on, oh my oh my!
For sometimes the riches aren't loud at all,
But hidden in quiet, they rise and they fall.

So here's to the hush, the calm and the cool,
Where the fortune unfolds, like a jester's tool.
For in silence lies humor, like treasures untold,
And the giggles of fortune are always pure gold.

The Weight of Unforgotten Moments

The scale in my kitchen weighs more than my cake,
It counts all the moments, the jests and the fake.
Each giggle and chuckle, each toe-tapping dance,
Hangs heavy and happy, like a stout little prance.

I tread lightly on memories soft,
As they wriggle and jive, they lift me aloft.
'More cake, less worry,' my heart does decree,
For laughter's the weight that sets my mind free.

We measure our lives with laughter as gold,
In weights of unforgotten, the stories unfold.
So next time you balance, just know you can sway,
With each giggle you gather, you brighten your day.

Forget the old scales of society's game,
For joy is the weight that requires no fame.
So let's dance on the scales, oh what a delight,
With laughter and moments, we'll soar through the night.

Enigmas Beneath This Skin

Beneath my skin a riddle lies,
Just like my socks, they're in disguise.
I ponder it while munching pie,
Is it a truth or just a lie?

With every wrinkle, a puzzle grows,
Like where do all my lost socks go?
They vanish fast, but never fret,
They're living wild, my secret pet!

A smile today, a frown tomorrow,
Tricks of light; I'm soaked in sorrow.
But who can tell beneath this grin?
The truth's a game I never win!

So laugh with me, don't shed a tear,
What's baked in mystery, have no fear.
A cheer for jokes and jumbled plight,
In the comedy of life, we're all uptight!

Ghosts of Unshed Tears

Cried a river, but no one saw,
They float on by without a flaw.
My ghosts are quirky, dressed in grey,
They dance around and make me sway.

Teardrops whisper, 'Don't you see?'
They shush me soft, then spill their glee.
With every droplet, tales unfold,
That tickle funny bones, so bold.

In shadows where the giggles lurk,
A smirk appears, oh what a quirk!
The haunting laugh of yesteryear,
Makes me chuckle through the fear.

So lift your cup to fleeting woes,
For laughter's light, it always flows.
Let's toast to tears that splash and play,
And guide us through the silliest day!

Underneath the Surface

Underneath I hide my quirks,
Like mismatched socks, they drive me berserk.
With subtle grins and hidden glee,
The jesters dance inside of me.

In every glance, a secret spark,
Like silly notes left in the park.
They snicker loud, but I pretend,
This layered humor never ends.

So take a peek and have a laugh,
My life's a jest, a funny staff.
In shadows thick where giggles dwell,
The hidden punchline casts a spell.

So let's embrace this playful skin,
'Cause who knows where the fun begins?
With every layer, a chuckle bursts,
In the comedy of secrets, the laughter thirsts!

Soft Cries of Buried Hearts

Softly tucked in, my heart does hide,
With jests and jives that abide.
It cries out sweet, yet laughs in jest,
Who knew it's such a silly quest?

Beneath the laughs, a sob or two,
Each giggle wraps a tear so blue.
Why whisper things that make me cringe?
When jokes abound, I swap and binge.

In secret corners, my laughter flares,
While solitude spins tangled snares.
But every trick, a wink I share,
Life's too short, I'll take a dare!

So here I stand with heart exposed,
With humor sharp, it is composed.
For every cry, a chuckle's born,
A waltz of secrets, life's soft scorn!

The Language of Lost Moments

In coffee spills and sticky notes,
We speak in whispers, silly anecdotes.
Forgotten socks and missing keys,
Life's puzzles solved with giggles and tease.

A dance with shadows, a wink of fate,
Tripping on truths that we celebrate.
We laugh at the mess, the jumbled page,
Each slip unveils a new kind of sage.

A tangled yarn, an un-typed text,
In moments lost, we find what's vexed.
The language of giggles, the wordplay of time,
In every misstep, we make it sublime.

With a chuckle shared, and a nudge so sly,
We find the brilliance in every "oh why?"
For secrets remain, but giggles we share,
In the hall of the forgotten, we dance without care.

Unraveled Confessions

In the laundry, secrets whirl and spin,
With every cycle, a tale to grin.
T-Shirts that speak of wild, late nights,
And mismatched socks that fought epic fights.

We wear our quirks like badges bright,
Each unraveling thread reveals sheer delight.
A coffee stain, a crumpled plan,
Life's oops moments, the best of the clan.

Confessions born in the fridge's hum,
Leftover pizza, a slice of fun.
Whispers of chocolate, late-night chats,
Writing our stories on napkins and hats.

Such whimsical truths in every mishap,
Memories catching in a ketchup trap.
What once was lost in the fray of haste,
Now grins at us from an unkempt place.

Paths Worn by Memory

On sidewalks cracked, we stroll and sway,
Each step remembering some child's play.
A lost balloon, a barking dog,
We haul our past like a happy fog.

The park bench sings of tales and chats,
Of secret plans, and haphazard spats.
Each path we blaze a dance of glee,
With every stumble, we're wild and free.

Bicycles ringing in the sun,
Chasing dreams, oh what fun!
Skinned knees and ice-cream runs,
Memory's paths are filled with puns.

With every photo's silent laugh,
We gather fragments, that silly half.
The worn-out routes, our laughter's trail,
In the gallery of time, we prevail.

Glimmers of the Forgotten

In dusty drawers, the treasures hide,
A mixture of ages, nowhere to bide.
Old mixtapes that scratch a heart's tune,
And love notes written by the light of the moon.

Each gleam of the past, a moment spry,
With rubber bands keeping dreams awry.
A rubber chicken, a smelly shoe,
Life shines bright in every hue.

Memories pop like bubbles, surreal,
Each popsicle stick a secret seal.
Here's to the glimmers that tickle our days,
In forgotten corners, we find our ways.

So let's share a laugh, our fondest hoard,
For in each odd memory, we're never bored.
With giggles and glances, the past can play,
Together we dance through a bright ballet.

Shadows of Forgotten Dreams

In the attic, dust bunnies play,
Old toys giggle at the fray.
A sock with holes, a tale to tell,
Of laundry days and a dryer spell.

Whispers come from the coffee pot,
"Remember me? That cozy spot?"
We share our laughs, lose track of time,
Chasing ghosts is quite sublime.

A hat with feathers, somewhat bold,
Claims to have stories left untold.
It dances around like it's still young,
Twisting and twirling, it's never done.

We toast to memories, slightly bent,
To the parts of us we never meant.
The past can giggle, waltz, and prance,
In shadows where the dreams still dance.

Echoes in the Silent Night

The moon whispers jokes, dim and bright,
As owls share punchlines, it's quite the sight.
Stars wink knowingly, cosmic jesters,
Reminding us we're all just investors.

A breeze tickles trees, they chuckle low,
While crickets compose a late-night show.
Each rustle and hum, a secret shared,
In the night's laughter, none are ensnared.

Comets flash by, making wishes pale,
While squirrels in capes steal the grand tale.
They leap through branches, so suave, so spry,
In shadows where forgotten dreams lie.

So here we sit, beneath the stars,
Daring the night with our old guitars.
In echoes of giggles, let's take flight,
For tomorrow to dance in the silent night.

Veils of Memory

Memory veils like curtains drawn,
Where socks and spoons have seemingly gone.
Each crease and fold of timeless lore,
Hiding treasures behind every door.

A sandwich made from years of fun,
With flavors mixed, is never done.
Pickles and laughter spread so thick,
Each bite reveals a quirky trick.

A jigsaw puzzle of silly faces,
Spills its secrets in hidden places.
One piece is missing, but who's to care?
We laugh as we spin tales in the air.

With every wrinkle, a giggle grows,
Funny stories that nobody knows.
In veils of memory, we commence,
The laughter echoes, our recompense.

The Unseen Paths We Tread

In the garden where wild things grow,
A snail's slow path puts on quite the show.
Shuffling along, it takes its time,
While frogs recite their quirky rhyme.

A pebble, a treasure, reflects the sun,
Whispers of giggles, oh what fun.
The flowers nod with petals bright,
To secrets shared in the soft twilight.

Bumblebees dance on paths unseen,
Hover like they're living a dream.
Chasing each other around the bloom,
In their buzzing world, there's always room.

So let's explore the unusual bends,
Where humor thrives and laughter blends.
In unseen paths, don't play it safe,
For the fun lies where the wild things waif.

The Passages We Walk Alone

In hallways thick with whispers,
We tiptoe past the doors.
Each one might hold a treasure,
Or just a pile of chores.

With every step we wander,
A giggle's on the breeze.
What lies behind each corner,
Could be a dance or tease.

The echoes of our choices,
Muffle laughter's sweet embrace.
We search for hidden voices,
In this peculiar place.

So stroll with me in silence,
In paths we make our own.
The joy is in the mystery,
Though we're still walking home.

Unspoken Words in Empty Rooms

In rooms where echoes linger,
Dust bunnies float like dreams.
We make our wild assumptions,
While plotting silly schemes.

A chair is dressed in shadows,
It grins at all we say.
The walls have heard our secrets,
And chuckle as we play.

A light bulb hums the chorus,
Of all the things we missed.
It's hard to find the courage,
To talk to a light mist.

Yet still we sit in silence,
And sip our cups of tea.
With unspoken words around us,
It's just you, the room, and me.

Stolen Glances and Silent Promises

Behind the plants we linger,
With eyes that spark like stars.
In crowded little corners,
We share our dreams from afar.

A wink, a nod, a chuckle,
In glances that ignite.
What's said in stolen moments,
Can linger into night.

With whispers in the hallway,
And smiles that break the rules.
We scribble on the margins,
Like playful, sneaky fools.

Let's dance upon the rooftops,
And make our silly plans.
With all these unkept promises,
We'll race with the slow fans.

The Enigma of Tomorrow

Tomorrow's just a riddle,
Wrapped in shiny foil.
We peek and pull the edges,
While hoping not to spoil.

Each dawn brings new surprises,
Some funny, some bizarre.
We're like unwritten novels,
With plot twists from afar.

The future holds our giggles,
And stumbles, oh so grand.
With every leap we take,
A twist slips from our hand.

We laugh at all the wonders,
As hours fly away.
In this enigma, we wander,
And hope for one more play.

Journeys Through the Unseen

In the attic, dust does dance,
Old trunks whisper, take a chance.
Maps to places never trod,
Hidden treasures? Oh my God!

A sock with holes, a shoe that squeaks,
Lost in laughter, time just peaks.
Forgotten crumbs of yesterday,
Tickling memories in a playful way.

Ciphers of Love

A note beneath the kitchen mat,
Scribbled hearts, it's where we sat.
Chocolate stains on old book spines,
Decipher me, with silly lines.

In coffee cups and whispered dreams,
Laughter bubbles like silly streams.
Decoding texts from way back when,
Our silly codes, we'll meet again.

Memories in Dust

Boxes stacked, a jumbled heap,
Relics from those nights we steep.
A feathered hat from years gone by,
Why did we think we'd learn to fly?

Dust bunnies in a grand ballet,
Swirling secrets, come out and play!
Forgotten joys, we giggle loud,
Stories spun, we're still so proud.

The Hidden Tapestry

In the garden, weeds and plots,
Weaving tales with tangled knots.
Silly shapes in colored threads,
Quirky stories fill our heads.

The quilt of chaos, life's design,
Patches sewed with love, divine.
Every stitch, a giggle burst,
Secrets woven, never cursed.

The Gardens of Unsaid Goodbyes

In gardens where goodbyes hide,
A gnome waves with a silly stride.
Leaves rustle with words unsaid,
While daisies laugh at the dread.

To plants we tell our secrets bold,
Yet they respond with tales of old.
Rabbits hop, with ears so keen,
Whispering the things we've seen.

So here we dig without a clue,
Harvesting what we never knew.
But every bloom brings a surprise,
Like birthdays in the strangest guise.

Beneath the sun, we roam and play,
While shadows giggle, come what may.
In this wild patch, we roam free,
With secrets sprouting like a tree.

The Clock That Keeps No Time

A clock on the wall ticks upside down,
It claims to know when we wear a frown.
Hands spinning wild in a frantic dance,
We wait for hours that never prance.

Big Ben's cousin is running late,
Sipping tea, it can't relate.
With every chime, it sets a stage,
For timeless tales of the silly age.

Seconds run by on a pogo stick,
Jumping again, they play a trick.
Minutes tumble like clumsy clowns,
Falling over time in jester gowns.

When noon arrives, we laugh aloud,
For who needs time in a silly crowd?
So toss your watches, let them shine,
In a world where clocks refuse to align.

Lanterns Lighting the Unseen

Lanterns sway on invisible strings,
Illuminating the wildest things.
Frogs in tuxedos leap and croak,
While shadow puppets blend and joke.

Each flicker reveals a quirky sight,
A dancing squirrel in mid-flight.
Whispers swirl in the evening mist,
As secrets play a guessing twist.

Fireflies escape with glowing charm,
Seductive lights, they raise alarm.
In this realm of the things we hide,
Jokes and giggles swell with pride.

So let your lanterns shine and gleam,
For what's unseen can still be deemed.
And with each laugh and sigh we share,
The shadows dance in bright, bold air.

Portraits of a Hidden Self

In frames on the wall, we grin so wide,
But behind them, we tend to hide.
A painting's smile that's far from true,
What secrets brush can spill anew?

Selfies stuck in frames of gold,
Reveal the funny stories told.
Each stroke whispers of deep desires,
While thoughts ignite like playful fires.

Behind the canvas, oh what a scene,
A cat is posing with a queen!
Cheeses and crackers, art supplies,
Cutouts laughing from other guys.

With every portrait, we reveal,
A slice of joy, a silly reel.
So hang them high, let laughter swell,
For hidden selves, who knows them well?

Remnants in the Echo Chamber

Whispers dance in the void, so sly,
Tickling the walls, a curious spy.
Faded laughs from the corners creep,
Echoes of secrets that can't quite sleep.

A sock with a story, lost without trace,
Tiptoeing around, what a silly chase!
Chasing a ghost that's really just fun,
Pretending it's missing, but is it just done?

The floorboards creak in a laughable tune,
Making mischief under the light of the moon.
Just a reminder that moments can jest,
And memories linger, but here they're a fest.

Laughter stored like confetti in air,
Each chuckle a lock, each giggle a pair.
In the echo chamber, joy cannot hide,
It leaps from the cracks, oh what a wild ride!

The Doorway to Possibilities

A door swings wide with a creaky refrain,
Promises peek through, like drops of rain.
What's behind it? Oh, who even knows,
Perhaps a garden where opportunity grows?

A sock puppet party, a dance of delight,
Mismatched shoes waltz under the starlight.
Open the door; it squeaks, it bends,
Here in this world, every quirk transcends.

With each step forward, you just might find,
A bunny in a waistcoat—go figure that kind!
Puddles of laughter flood the old floor,
Life's just a giggle behind every door.

The hallway extends through time and through space,
Tripping on wonder, you quicken your pace.
Mysteries beckon, they laugh and they tease,
In this doorway of chance, the soul sings with ease!

The Silence of Old Letters

Dusty envelopes stacked high like a tower,
Each a magician, hiding a power.
Witty remarks sealed with a kiss,
Who knew such silence could come with such bliss?

Postmarks reveal where the fun may roam,
Paris to Poughkeepsie, so far from home.
Each line a riddle, each word has a grin,
Sneaky little secrets tucked safely within.

Deciphering ink with a smirk on my face,
Who knew John's cat had such terrible taste?
In the stillness, the laughter's not lost,
Old letters abound, at no matter the cost.

Finding joy in the scribbles so bold,
A time travel joke waiting to unfold.
In silence, old letters are anything but tame,
A chorus of chuckles, oh what a fame!

The Haunting of Secret Places

What lurks in the nooks where shadows play?
Chasing giggles that never decay.
A hat with a tale, an old chair that squeaks,
In secret places, the funny still speaks.

Ghosts in the cupboard sip tea and conspire,
Trading old jokes, their spirits on fire.
A broom in the corner twirls on its own,
Sweeping away every sigh, every groan.

The attic is filled with whispers and dreams,
Where nothing's as simple as just what it seems.
Tales of the past with a wink and a nod,
Just call upon them—oh, they're never abroad!

In the crevices lie giggles like charms,
A phantom that dances in whimsical arms.
Unlocking the humor in all that was lost,
In secret places, laughter is the cost!

Encrypted in Time

In a jar beneath the bed,
Forgotten socks and tales unsaid.
Time encrypted, secrets mime,
Laundry whispers, oh so prime!

We stumble o'er the dusty past,
Each memory a quirky cast.
Tick-tock giggles in the night,
As we juggle wrong and right!

The clock's a joker, always late,
Donuts stolen off my plate.
With every tick, a laugh we share,
Time's rich tapestry laid bare.

Yet in this funny, tangled spree,
Life's oddities dance, wild and free.
So twist the locks and break the mold,
For every secret, there's a fold!

Lanterns in the Attic

Up in the attic, cobweb town,
Lanterns flicker, dust motes drown.
Forgotten treasures full of glee,
Mismatched socks and odd esprit!

A squeaky floorboard, what a tease,
Rats gossip like the worst of bees.
One shoe laughs, the other sighs,
As dust bunnies plot their goodbyes!

They'd tell jokes if only they could,
In a language understood.
Each creak and crack a punchline tight,
Under the moon's gentle light.

So let's wade through these memory floods,
Finding humor where it buds.
In the attic's quirky twist,
Life plays tricks, we can't resist!

The Gatekeeper's Lament

At the gate sits a goofball sprite,
With popcorn kernels and a kite.
'Secrets here? Oh please, how grand!'
He chuckles while waving his hand.

With each lock clicks a jolly tune,
As he mocks the bright-eyed moon.
'Why guard what's best left untold?
With laughter, build a fortress bold!'

A riddle here, a giggle there,
The gatekeeper dances without a care.
His belly shakes, a jelly roll,
As he guards the spirit and the soul!

So join him in this bumbling quest,
Unlocking secrets, jesting best.
In the twilight's funny glow,
Forget the keys, let laughter flow!

Unraveled Threads of Fate

Threads of fate, a tangled mess,
Swirls of fluff, I must confess.
Stitch my dreams with giggles sweet,
While cats walk in with nimble feet.

With every twist, a prank is born,
A sock puppet sings, all forlorn.
Old tales unravel in our hands,
As laughter echoes across the lands.

Mismatched buttons, a quirky clasp,
As fate's wild jokes, we try to grasp.
We stitch and laugh, or pull and tug,
In a dance that makes reality shrug.

So let's entwine the funny thread,
In life's fabric, bright and spread.
No locks or keys can hide the cheer,
In this tapestry, we hold dear!

Corners of the Mind

In the attic of thoughts, dust bunnies prance,
Old memories jive, they all love to dance.
You might find a sock, or a lost old key,
But mostly just giggles, floating with glee.

Underneath stacks of books, lies a shoe,
That once traveled roads, both old and new.
It whispers of journeys, a traveler's plight,
Teasing the brain, let's go fly a kite!

Comics and doodles, stuck on the walls,
Each paper cut monster sweetly recalls.
A crayon drawing, of a cat in a hat,
Quirky escapades of a curious brat.

In corners we chuckle, no reason to pout,
Every locked box has a key tucked about.
So rummage and giggle, take a long peek,
The heart's best treasures, are often quite cheeky.

The Puzzle of Forgotten Places

A map once unfolded, with lines all askew,
Showing the spots where laughter just grew.
The park with the swings, the pond with the ducks,
Where we traded our pennies for silly good lucks.

Forgotten ice cream shops, where flavors collide,
In sticky handprints, our childhood confides.
Scoops of pure chaos, drips on our shirts,
With giggles that echoed, and motherly flirts.

Paths that meander, through wild grassy fields,
Where we shared secrets, our hearts truly healed.
Bees buzzed our tales, as the sun kissed our skin,
In nooks of nostalgia, let madness begin.

So shuffle these pieces, let laughter explore,
For hidden places still open their door.
With silly assumptions, and bright twinkling eyes,
We'll find treasure maps covered in sweet, tasty pies.

Echoes of Laughter and Tears

In the garden of giggles, where daisies bloom bright,
A sprinkle of sunshine fills up the night.
Each chuckle, a petal, each sigh, a leaf,
In this whimsical world, there's often no grief.

We dance with our shadows, slapping the ground,
Mixing our giggles with joy that we found.
Between fits and flops, the fun never ends,
For laughter's the glue that forever transcends.

Sometimes we tumble, a slip on the way,
Falling so hard, we can't help but sway.
With moans of our falls, we will snicker and cheer,
Because mixed with the fumbling, is joy for a year!

So cast out your troubles, let silly reign free,
In echoing chambers of wild jubilee.
Unlocking the moments, the bittersweet seams,
We wear laughter like crowns, while dreaming our dreams.

Paths of Forgotten Whispers

In the woods of our stories, where whispers take flight,
Paths twist and twirl, in the thick of the night.
Old tales float around like leaves in the breeze,
We stumble on memories, like cheese on a tease.

Each rustle a giggle hidden behind,
With critters conspiring, they plot and unwind.
Rabbits with secrets, and owls in disguise,
Watch as the unknown catches us by surprise.

The trail twists around, leading steps that we trace,
Through giggly good jokes and a daydreaming race.
A mix of the silly and poignant, we find,
In whispers forgotten, we're never confined.

So journey through shadows, where laughter's the map,
With whimsical echoes, there's no time to nap.
In paths of nostalgia, let's dance 'round the fires,
Unlocking our whimsy, igniting our desires.

Veils of Yesterday

Hidden under blankets, dust and care,
Memories whisper, but I'm unaware.
Old photos giggle, faces with flair,
Secrets of ages dance in the air.

In jars of jam, truths pickle and peel,
Pranks played on me—what a wobbly wheel!
I never age, just a clever conceal,
Every missed birthday, another surreal.

Old shoes in the closet, where have they gone?
They've shimmied away, in a boogie so strong.
I swear I saw them at the break of dawn,
Chasing their youth like a nostalgic song.

Yet with a chuckle, I'll raise a glass,
To those faded memories, oh, what a class!
In lighthearted truth, let the past amass,
For today's full of giggles, let worries bypass.

Silent Letters in the Drawer

In drawers so deep, where whispers reside,
Letters lie dormant, with secrets to bide.
Each one a story, with a grin and a slide,
Laughing at love notes that time tried to hide.

The ink is a puzzle, in loops and in curls,
Tales of odd crushes, of boys and of girls.
With paper airplanes, and memories in swirls,
Those silent communications send giggling twirls.

Oh, the romance of tea stains and smeared lines,
Unfolding the paper, oh how it defines!
Each crease holds a chuckle, where awkwardness shines,
In long-forgotten letters, where laughter intertwines.

So here's to the moments that tickle the fates,
Dancing with ghosts and outdated plates.
In a drawer full of letters, life deliberates,
What's silent today once buzzed with debates.

Treasures of the Untold

In the attic's corners, treasures sit tight,
Dusty old boxes, but oh what a sight!
A rubber chicken tangled with toys that's just right,
With giggles and shivers, they bring sheer delight.

Beneath the old blankets, a trumpet offbeat,
A forgotten parade on these creaking feet.
Each treasure awakens a memory sweet,
As echoes of laughter and mischief repeat.

Oh, what a spectacle, odd trinkets unfold,
Unearthing lost stories, some silly, some bold.
A jester's hat lying next to some gold,
In the vault of the past, where wonders behold.

So I dive into boxes, and pull out the fun,
In treasures of yesteryear, laughter's begun.
Every piece is a puzzle, every thread is spun,
And in these memories, I'm never outdone.

The Voice of Faded Dreams

Hush now, gently, come gather around,
A voice from the past, now lost, it has found.
Faded dreams chuckle, on memories profound,
With tales of mishaps and laughs that resound.

Once in a while, they peek from the mist,
With playful reminders, long twirls that persist.
Like socks in the wash, or a long-forgotten tryst,
Every giggle and snicker, whimsically kissed.

From journeys of yore, where all life was chic,
The blunders and bluffs, so charmingly unique.
In the garden of laughter, they silently seek,
To dance in the daylight, with joy they sneak.

So listen up closely, let the echoes hum,
With a wink and a grin, oh what cheers they become!
In the tapestry woven from quiet and fun,
These voices of dreams, never truly outrun.

Windows to the Unexplored

A window with curtains bright and bold,
Hides a world of stories yet untold.
Peeking through, I see a cat,
Wearing glasses, looking quite phat.

Behind the glass, a dance unfolds,
Pigeons gossip as a story unfolds.
A snail in a tie, he's on his way,
To a meeting where no one will stay.

What treasures lie in the dusty nook?
Perhaps a lost sock, or an old book.
Each creak of the floor is a giggle,
As the shadows around me start to wiggle.

So lift the sash and take a peep,
You never know what secrets will leap!
With laughter abound and quirks galore,
These windows will share so much more!

Pathways to the Untold

Follow the path where the wild weeds grow,
Frogs in tuxedos ready for the show.
Watch where you step, there's puddles to splash,
Look at that squirrel—it just made a dash!

The signposts all point in every way,
One says 'Left', the other goes 'Yay!'.
Choose your direction, it's all a bluff,
As the trees chuckle—this is their stuff.

A rabbit with wisdom, sporting a hat,
Tells you the tales of his grandpa's spat.
His carrots are tales, juicy and ripe,
Sipping on tea, the best kind of hype.

So wander along these whimsical trails,
With laughter and giggles, let's follow the tales.
The pathways are winding, the stories are bold,
Adventure awaits, let the jokes unfold!

The Guardian of Forgotten Truths

In an attic dusty, lives a wise old chair,
Guarding the secrets of glittery hair.
Once a kingdom of lost socks and fluff,
Now it just laughs—a treasure trove tough!

The guardian chuckles, adjusting his specs,
Telling tales that confuse even Rex.
"Did you hear about the fish who can sing?
He won the contest, held by a king!"

Amidst old boxes the memories wane,
Like the dusty vase that holds only rain.
Each trinket whispers of laughter and cheer,
The guardian chuckles, "All's well, my dear."

So listen closely, as he spins the lore,
Of dances and prances behind every door.
There's magic in each forgotten fact,
With humor entwined, truth's never lacked!

Raindrops on Secret Paths

Pitter-patter, raindrops chase,
Frogs wear boots, keeping pace.
Each drop giggles as it slinks,
Into the puddles with silly winks.

Dancing on cobblestones slick and bright,
While worms wiggle in sheer delight.
The skies peek through with sunlit grins,
"Hey! Who said that rain's no fun?"

Splat! A raindrop lands on my nose,
A secret message, the wind then knows.
"Follow this path, it leads to a feast,
Where cupcakes are plenty, not just the least!"

So splash through the puddles, dance in the rain,
Each drop a note in the sweetest refrain.
The joy in the journey, oh so bizarre,
In every raindrop, lies a glimpse of the star!

Whispers in the Attic

In the attic's dusty hall,
Old toys gossip, having a ball.
They swap tales of playtime's heyday,
While dust bunnies wiggle and sway.

A teddy bear with a crooked grin,
Claims he's the king where dust begins.
A drum speaks softly, 'I once was loud!'
While the doll dreams, feeling quite proud.

The old clock ticks, sharing its luck,
'I've seen them all, and they were struck!'
But who'll believe a clock's tall tale?
With whispers and chuckles, they set sail.

So in that attic, laughter ignites,
As secrets take flight on friendly nights.
With every creak and cheeky wink,
They store those memories, or so we think.

Echoes of the Unsaid

In a room where echoes get shy,
A shoe squeaks softly, 'Oh, my, my!'
It whispers tales of cobbled streets,
And a dance-off with mismatched feet.

The mirror chuckles, it knows the truth,
Reflecting the joys of our silly youth.
It hides a smirk for all the near misses,
When dresses fell in party kisses.

A sombrero sits, feeling quite grand,
Claiming it's the star of the band.
'They never invited me on that ride!'
It sways with pride, though it cannot hide.

As night falls, they share a laugh,
Echoes of joy—a silly gaffe.
Yes, those unsaid things—so much fun,
In the vibrant dance of a setting sun.

The Key Beneath the Floorboard

Beneath the floorboard, a key does hide,
It giggles softly with secret pride.
It dreams of doors that won't ever swing,
And of mysteries, oh, what fun they bring!

The old cat watches, with one eye closed,
Pretending it's wise, but secretly dozed.
'That key's for the treasure we store for snacks,'
It mutters and yawns, while dreaming of rats.

Nearby, a spider spins tales of her own,
Of hidden delights within her cozy home.
'I could teach you a thing or two, my friend,'
She winks at the key, 'If you'd just pretend!'

As sunbeams dance and shadows play loud,
Secrets are silly when shared with a crowd.
The key may be lost, but it sure knows how,
To unlock laughter from here and from now.

Shadows of the Unseen

In the corner, shadows play peek-a-boo,
With the lamp's warm glow, they glint and skew.
They whisper secrets, soft as a sigh,
Making shadows giggle, flit, and fly.

A sock puppet cries, 'I'm not just a mate!'
He declares himself king of the cluttered state.
While a shadowy cat makes a graceful leap,
Promising secrets that she'll never keep.

The rug rolls over, feeling quite blessed,
As crumbs from last night settle and rest.
'You missed a party! Where were you, dear?'
The dust motes flutter, just glad to be here!

So in this room, where shadows delight,
Funny antics unfold in the soft moonlight.
Even unseen, they bask in the fun,
Life's little chuckles, for everyone!

Chambers of Quiet Yearning

In a room filled with socks, my hopes do reside,
With mismatched dreams, they wriggle and glide.
The echoes of laughter escape from the seams,
As I search for the lost pair of whimsical schemes.

A cat on the sofa, he knows all the tales,
Of chasing the shadows and colorful snails.
His secretive purring is filled with delight,
While I ponder the mysteries of dust bunnies' flight.

Behind every closet, a treasure awaits,
Or at least a dust bunny that wobbles and mates.
Oh, to find joy in the quirks of each day,
With a wink and a nudge, they're never far away.

In the chambers of yearning, let laughter unfold,
For the wackiest stories are the ones rarely told.
With each silly twist, life's laughter ignites,
As we dance through the chaos and bask in the lights.

Clues in the Dusty Corners

There's a map made of crumbs on my kitchen floor,
Trailing like pirates, who endlessly explore.
The dog sniffs for treasures in each little crack,
Wondering if lettuce is what I'll bring back.

In the attic sits Grandma, with tales yet to spin,
Her knitting is tangled, but oh, the grin!
With each twist of the yarn, a story unspools,
Of mischievous kids and their elaborate rules.

Beneath layers of dust, with some cheer and dismay,
The secrets we've whispered come out to play.
A sock stuffed with laughter, a spoon carved with pride,
Turns dust into gold when the world's on our side.

So let's dust off our dreams and give them a spin,
For treasures are hiding, and mischief can win.
With giggles and twirls, let playtime commence,
In corners of laughter, we break down the fence.

The Diary of Hidden Journeys

I found an old journal beneath a damp sock,
Filled with doodles and schemes that could tickle a rock.
Each scribble a voyage, each line a new thrill,
Of pirates and dragons, it's quite the raw deal.

The pages are folded, some stuck with old jam,
Fruits of adventure, or maybe green spam?
But the laughter still echoes from trips long ago,
Where I battled a llama—all in a faux glow.

Oh, the journeys we hide between crumbs of the bread,
Where the pineapple danced with the peanut butter spread.
With a wink and a giggle, reality blurs,
As I sail through the pages where laughter is stirred.

So let's pen our adventures in all colors so bright,
With paths lined in giggles; our stories take flight.
For in every misstep, there's fun to be had,
And in pages of folly, we'll never be sad.

Fragments of What Wasn't Said

There's a note on the fridge, held tight by a magnet,
It whispers of snacks with a silent bragnet.
A half-eaten sandwich, a lonely chip bag,
Declares all forgotten—the hops and the hag.

In corners where voices once roared like a storm,
The remnants of laughter take on a new form.
A slapstick banana peel grins from the floor,
Reminding us all what the giggles were for.

The whispers we stifle, the jokes left to rust,
Are better than treasures, for laughter's a must.
They tickle our minds in the quirkiest ways,
While we cherish the fragments of yesterday's plays.

So here's to the whispers, the comedy gold,
To each secret chuckle that's ever been told.
In the echoes of mirth, we'll dance with glee,
For there's magic in fragments that sets our hearts free.

Gilded Secrets of the Past

In a treasure chest, so very grand,
Old socks and toys, a mismatched band.
Golden coins from a cereal prize,
With every find, a new surprise!

Dust bunnies dance with jubilant glee,
In corners where no one can see.
Forgotten cookies from last fall's stash,
Their crunch is a memory, a delightful crash!

What's that smell? Oh, it's just me,
Dressed in yesterday's mystery.
With each odd item, a chuckle we raise,
Gilded secrets from younger days!

The Scribe of Untold Stories

A quill pen nestled in an old drawer,
With tales of snacks and a muffin war.
"Who stole my cookie?" the scribe will cry,
While we giggle and wonder why!

Wrinkled napkins with scribbles galore,
Of mishaps and laughter, they surely store.
Whispers of pranks that never grow old,
In a language of doodles, mischief unfolds!

The history kept in our crumpled trash,
From birthday cakes to a dog named Flash.
As we read them, we fancy the fun,
The scribe of our stories has surely won!

Treasures Buried Deep

In the backyard lies a pirate's delight,
An old shoe with treasures, what a sight!
Missing socks and a toy belt buckle,
All buried deep, who could resist the chuckle?

Maps drawn in crayon, leading the way,
To find the buried gems that brighten our day.
Goldfish crackers and candy wrappers too,
Oh, what a fortune, what joy anew!

As we dig through dirt, laughter erupts,
Over a jellybean jar where candy's corrupt.
In this treasure hunt, we find what we seek,
As joy springs forth, unique and antique!

The Labyrinth Within

In the attic's maze, I lose my mind,
Echoes of laughter are the best kind.
Tangled in yarn, and oh, what a mess,
With every twist, there's joy, I confess!

Old dolls with stories stare with surprise,
Got mismatched hats and glittery eyes.
Cobwebs hang like tales unspooled,
In a labyrinth where our humor ruled!

Each pathway leads to a room of charm,
With treasures that smirk at each little harm.
Inside this maze, oh, what can we find?
Gems of giggles tangled in the mind!

www.ingramcontent.com/pod-product-compliance
Lightning Source LLC
Chambersburg PA
CBHW051631160426
43209CB00004B/596